What People are Saying About The Unimagined Awakening

"A magical journey of inspiration and human perseverance, told by a magnificent, powerful, and gracious being. Janie shares in a way that comes truly from the heart and moves the soul. A definite must-read."

~ JB Owen
Founder and CEO of Ignite
www.igniteyou.life

"Janie J gives the reader a snapshot of her life as it unfolded and her spiritual journey began. Follow along as you learn just how much her life changed and affected every aspect of her being. Be inspired to start on your own soul path."

Don Boyer
Film Producer
www.BeyondtheSecret.com

"If you want to find answers to those pesky life issues that have plagued you for years, Janie's book will teach you how to learn your life lessons, access your own higher intuitive guidance, and get out of your comfort zone so you can have the life you want. Charming and succinct, The Unimagined Awakening is a wonderful guide to the next stage of your soul's journey!"

Dr. Gary Salyer
Transformational Relationship Mentor, Speaker & Author
www.garysalyer.com

"Rather daring! This story takes us beyond what we might expect. It was fascinating to watch the massive transformation - a true transformation - spiritually and lifewise. A story worth reading and experiencing!"

Keith Garrick
Author and Creator of The Life University
www.thelifeuniversity.us

"Janie's message comes to you fresh from a realm beyond our everyday perception. This is why she was chosen to deliver it to us. Only read if you want to awaken, and if you want to awaken, read every word!"

~ Yoram Baltinester
The Personal Development Samurai
International Best-selling Author
www.HeyYoram.com

"Janie Jurkovich is so spot on in how we land here with lessons. Can we learn our lessons faster? Yes, we can, by paying attention, and the wisdom of this book in your hands right now will help you clue into the lessons handed to us ever so subtly."

~ Rusti L. Lehay
Book Coach/Empathic Editor
International Best-selling Author

"Janie reminds us that Universal Truths can be accessed by reaching peaceful states of being and allowing divine information to ooze through the veil. I just adore how her intuition has brought this great gift into the collective consciousness!"

Benjamin Ivanowski
Author, RN, Hawk Medicine Healer

The Unimagined Awakening

The Unimagined Awakening

My Journey from Spiritually-Starved Workaholic
to Connecting to "All That Is"

JANIE JURKOVICH

The Unimagined Awakening
Janie Jurkovich

2nd Edition
Copyright © 2022

Motivate Enterprise
3200 East Guasti Road #112
Ontario, California 91761

ISBN: 978-1-7369476-5-4

All rights reserved. No part of this publication may be reproduced, stored in a retrieval system, or transmitted in any form or by any means without the written permission of the publisher.

The Unimagined Awakening is sold with the understanding that neither the publisher nor the author is engaged to render any type of psychological, legal, or any other kind of professional advice. The content is the sole expression and opinion of its author. No warranties or guarantees are expressed or implied by the content herein.

Neither the publisher nor the author shall be liable for any physical, psychological, emotional, financial, or commercial damages, including, but not limited to, special, incidental, consequential, or other damages. You are responsible for your own choices, actions, and results.

Author's Photo by Signature Creations Photography
Cover Image estivillml / 123RF
Printed in the United States of America

Learn How to Connect to Experience Your Own Unimagined Awakening

Are you here to change your life for the better?

Are you here to upgrade your existence?

Are you here to help move mankind to a higher level of consciousness that is in line with what our Creator envisioned?

Get the Connect to Transform Process

Free Instant Download

Go to

www.TheNewIAmMovement.com/transform

to learn how to connect to others, your higher self, your spirit guides, the Ascended Masters, and the universal intelligence.

Table of Contents

Acknowledgments 13
Introduction 15
A Burning Desire for Change 19
Receiving the First Download 23
Accepting My Assignments 27
Traveling Through My Comfort Zone 33
Acknowledging My Final Mission 41
Connecting and Asking My Spirit Guides 45
Uncovering Past Lives Through Love 49
Exploring The New I AM Document, Volume I 55
Unlocking the Key to Ascension 61
BONUS: BOOK EXCERPT 67
Lesson 1 - The Purpose 71
Join The New I AM Movement 73
About Janie Jurkovich 75

Acknowledgments

I would like to thank Don Boyer for his mentorship in helping bring this book to life. With the release of my episode on the Amazon Prime series of "The Awakening," this book seemed to be the perfect pairing to aid one in the understanding of mediumship. His team has been instrumental in this process, for which I am most thankful.

My creative team, composed of photographer Wonda Correia of Signature Creations and designer Ellie Dote of Ellie Girl, was able to capture the essence of a peaceful setting where my spiritual life began.

It takes all of us to show the ways to lift humanity higher, and Beth Bridges, my editor and marketer extraordinaire, is a perfect example of how we all work together. She tirelessly reviewed every page of this book, prompting me to clarify my story so others could more easily understand how it could, indeed, be possible. I appreciate her enthusiasm and interest in this project.

My spirit guides have repeatedly told me, "We are all but cogs in the wheels of creation, each doing our own part to move mankind forward." I am fortunate to have been touched by these wonderful beings as part of my journey.

Introduction

This book describes the journey that led me to write, or, more accurately, transcribe a series of 100 lessons from ascended masters. Even though I had begun my spiritual journey, I was a "babe in the spiritual woods," so to speak. I had no understanding of what was truly possible in this thing called "life."

Recently divorced and in my sixties with limited religious training, I was not the type of person one might expect to receive a divine download. I did not spend my time sitting around in the lotus position, reciting "Om." I didn't smoke pot when I was in college (or now). I hadn't read any of the classic spirituality books.

Instead, I was a hard-working, college-educated woman who did not have time to even ponder the meaning of life. My business background was in developing, building, and leasing warehouse properties. During my marriage, I spent many years accompanying my former husband around the globe for his military career. Later, we raised two children.

When my 35-year marriage abruptly came to an end, I started to seek answers.

Once I opened the pandora's box of a spiritual life, I became an earnest learner and quickly absorbed my lessons. My spiritual education continues even now as it is something that is never really finished. We are all works in progress.

The New I AM Document, Volume I is a transcribed discourse received from ascended masters in another plane or dimension. I *felt* these words, rather than *heard* them.

The book presents 100 of the most important lessons that mankind is here to learn. These are life-changing lessons written in simple language with illustrative stories.

It is intended to be a timeless and profound publication. **Once mankind adopts these teachings and learns to live by them, the face of humanity will be forever changed!** This book is *that* powerful!

You might wonder how a divine download could "magically" occur. Well, there is much more to the story, and that is the purpose of *this* book.

Come along and join my amazing journey that shows how I went from being a spiritually-starved workaholic to discovering how to tap into my intuition and accept my gifts, to where I am today, using this knowledge to help humanity live their best lives.

By sharing my journey, I am hopeful that others will be encouraged to take the plunge into the spiritual world and discover just what *their* lives are meant to be. You are urged to read this book with an open mind, an open heart, and the eagerness of a child so that you, too, can learn to embrace all that we as a human species can be.

Ultimately, the purpose of this book is to bring you a greater understanding of this adventure we are all on—the adventure of our lifetimes.

Janie Jurkovich (Janie J)

Chapter One

A Burning Desire for Change

M y journey began at age 60, after I separated from my husband.

I knew my life needed fixing.

I was certain I didn't want to live the rest of my life stuck on that hamster wheel of never-ending work with no time to enjoy life.

This very strong *burning desire* led me to seriously focus on trying to figure things out. I knew there had to be a way.

I knew there was more to life than there appeared to be. And I was *determined* to figure out what it was and how to live my best life!

I became aware of my own intuition by reading a book on the subject and trying to apply the practices. I developed a daily ritual of meditation, reflective time, and mindfulness as a way to quiet my mind.

Then I started hearing inner voices which would guide me and make suggestions on what I could do to improve my life. These little check-ins were an everyday occurrence. I would spend from 30 minutes to two hours a day trying to focus on what I needed to do to turn my life around—trying to determine the concrete steps I needed to take.

I read more books and listened to podcasts. I asked for guidance, and the inner voices (whom I later called my spirit guides) would respond. I was open to ideas and kept asking questions, such as, "How do I figure this out?"

When I would find out one little bit of information, I would ask, "How do I figure this next thing out?" I also wondered if this was normal behavior because it was certainly not anything I had ever heard of or experienced.

Fortunately, the Universe had recently sent a new friend to me through a networking group. She was older than I and a bit disheveled and somewhat ostracized by others in our networking group because she didn't fit the polished, professional vision one might expect.

However, she was so nice and kind. She willingly took me under her wing. Since I had few friends, this was a welcomed treat, and I eagerly took her up on her offer of friendship.

I confided in her about the voices, who seemingly guided me when I needed help. When I would learn the next thing, I would ask, "Well, what about this? Or what about that?" And then the next book, podcast, or article on the

Internet, whatever it was, would seem to miraculously appear to help guide me, much in the way she had.

She explained that we all have guides that help us, and it's a matter of tapping into them.

She explained things such as different levels, sort of like a multi-story building, and each level was a different place where we could connect with others. This made no sense to me, but I kept an open mind.

I remember making a drawing on a napkin at the restaurant while we were eating lunch and later putting the napkin on my desk so I could refer to it and try to let the concept sink in. Later, I came to understand she was trying to explain different dimensions and how we can connect to spiritual beings in those dimensions.

In order to believe this paradigm, I had to first understand the concept that I was not my body; instead, I was a spiritual being.

What a big "a ha" moment. I remember being introduced to the quote by Pierre Teilhard de Chardin: "We are not human beings having a spiritual experience. We are spiritual beings having a human experience."

Fully understanding this concept was a bit difficult for me. The process took time, effort, and lots of diligence. It was through the constant asking of questions that things seemed to really spur along.

As a result, I was about to receive my first download.

Chapter Two

Receiving the First Download

Within a few months of starting this journey, something interesting happened, but I hid it from everyone.

Until, one day, it "just popped out." I revealed "live" on the air that I had received a divine download.

Oddly enough, it was during a religious podcast with two good friends. They didn't bat an eye at my startling disclosure, which made me feel at ease. (See how the Universe continues to send us just the right people when we need them?)

Here's what I told them.

After months of diligently trying to figure out how to have a better life, a cascade of information suddenly came to me while I was driving. It was like the sky had opened up and all the things I'd read, learned, and heard about were suddenly pouring into my head.

This information contained the answers to my never-ending questions of how to have a better life. And it was really great information!

I knew that I must write it down or I would soon forget. So I pulled over to the side of the road and wrote for 40 minutes.

The information consisted of small steps that anyone could take to get their life going on the right track. Looking back, I now realize these are the same steps that others, many others, have written in books, presented in seminars, and tried to teach. But it was really big news in my world at the time.

I eventually accepted that this had been a divine download!

I decided to write a blog on two social media platforms, where I would post one of the helpful tips each week. I did not have the blogs fully written. I didn't even know exactly what I was going to say. I just merely had the topics and the tips for about 30 steps to take to improve one's life.

So, I made it a goal. I made a commitment that every Thursday night before I went to bed I would post on social media.

What happened afterwards was quite amazing to me. I didn't think anybody would read what "little old me" wrote on social media, but after a while, friends in my networking groups started mentioning to me how the tips helped them. They would share my suggestions with others, and they would *all* be looking forward to my next tip.

This was just the encouragement and validation I needed, so I continued until all 30 steps were revealed.

The first tip was to get enough sleep. Once my ex-husband left, I finally got enough sleep (after about 20 years of being sleep deprived). I realized I had been living in a fog and that one simply cannot make good decisions if they aren't getting enough sleep.

Getting enough sleep was literally the most life-changing thing I could have ever done. You see, I was just going through the motions of working hard and doing what society said I should do.

I would have never woken up to the possibilities this life holds or what it could be otherwise.

As important as sleep was, there was another practice that was imperative for me on my spiritual journey. That practice was meditation.

At the time, I didn't know much about meditation, how to do it, or even *why* to do it. I didn't follow a certain protocol, use a specific mantra, or even sit cross-legged. (Who can sit like that for long periods of time, anyway?)

But I did learn how to relax and calm my thoughts by following the exercises in the intuition book I had been reading, called *Practical Intuition* by Laura Day.

Once I let go of all the worries and pressing tasks that were filling my head, I was able to accomplish something that had never occurred. I was able to *listen*.

At first, I was hesitant to include meditation as one of the main strategies in my book because I thought I would get a lot of backlash for recommending something so "far out." It was only because of the great changes I experienced in my own life that I decided to include it.

Meditation turned out to be the key to the rest of my journey.

Chapter Three

Accepting My Assignments

It took several months to finish writing and posting all the weekly blogs on social media. I was proud of myself and satisfied after completing that goal.

However, a year and a half later, during my morning meditation, my spirit guides told me quite clearly that I needed to write a book to help others live a better life using the same steps I had shared on social media.

I accepted the assignment.

Then they gave me a one-month deadline, which was probably a good thing because I might still be wallowing in that task!

The draft of *Live the Life You Have Imagined* was done at the stroke of midnight thirty days later.

I was quite pleased with myself for completing the task of writing my first book. It wasn't published yet. and that would still take some time; but I had met the deadline given by my guides.

Resting on my laurels was not an option because as soon as the first book was finished, my spirit guides told me to write another book. And once again, they gave me a 30-day deadline!

This book was to be the story of my journey of divorcing later in life and not just surviving, but thriving, to serve as an example to other women. My story is meant to be humorous, and hopefully, inspirational. The gist of it is that I *did* make it.

Honestly, my biggest worry when I split with my former husband was keeping my dream home. It might seem silly or frivolous to others, but because I followed him during his military career, I waited years to have the house I wanted in the country. We had been settled for 15 years, and the home still hadn't come to fruition. He had no plans, so I decided to build it myself once I had the financial means.

When I inherited the funds to start on that adventure, I invited him along, and he said he was on board. However, six years into it, he was *not* on board. He was not happy. He basically turned into a grumpy old man, and whatever was missing in his life was somehow my fault.

Despite my best efforts in working three jobs, maintaining the house, and doing all the cooking, cleaning, and bookkeeping, alas, it just wouldn't work.

When he left, I wasn't so worried about him leaving, rather, I wished him well and knew that he needed some help on his challenges. I was more worried about myself.

How would I keep from becoming a bag lady? How could I keep my home that I so dearly loved? How was I going to dig myself out of debt, keep my home, and maintain my sanity without working so hard?

Well, I figured it out through the tips in my first book, but I also showed myself how tenacious I was and how much perseverance I actually had. I'm not kidding—it was tough!

There were times when I was so mad at God, mostly for making all the things around my house stop functioning. I even shouted out to God and said, "If this is a sign that I need a man in my life, I am not giving up!" After that, things calmed down a bit; it was like a test—at least, it *felt* like a test.

Once again, I barely met the deadline of 30 days. On the last day, I finished the rough draft of the book, *Single and Sixty*, thinking all is well; I've done my job.

But that was not the case! I was given yet *another* task by my spirit guides. This time, the book was to be called *The Single Woman's Guide to Happiness*.

I think the purpose of that book was to show me that I could be happy on my own and didn't need a man. It was also important to share this message with other women who might think their lives were over because their husbands divorced them, left them, or died. Whatever the circumstances for being alone later in life, they needed to know they were *enough* on their own. So once again, I wrote that book as directed.

Next, I set about to publish these books, but it was not a direct route.

At first, I continued to work as a new commercial real estate broker. I'm embarrassed to admit this, but I kept trying to chase the almighty dollar. I was intent on working real estate deals. I would accept or take on the most difficult deals. I would work diligently, yet, despite my efforts, they would not result in closed transactions.

Finally, I just said, "The heck with it. God wants these books published. God can figure out the money!" I decided to stop working in real estate and make do with my investment income and just wing it. I thought, if worse comes to worst, and God wants me to, I will sell my dream house and move into an apartment, but *I will* get these books published!

Thankfully, I did not have to resort to the drastic measure of selling my home, but you can see the depth of my commitment.

A few months before I turned 65, I formally retired from real estate to focus on my writing and publishing career.

I knew I needed help to get these books published. I considered a couple of people. I even asked my guides for help. They said the person I selected would be a good fit, and she was!

Once I hired her, she promptly made me rewrite, edit, and improve the books, which was probably a good idea. This process took quite a bit of time. Then she helped me design, lay out, and get the books published. I found out there was much more to publishing a book than just writing it!

Early on, we decided it was more trouble than it was worth to hire a publishing company, even if we could find one. So I decided to self-publish, which was then possible due to Amazon's print-on-demand capabilities.

After I self-published the first book, *Live the Life You Have Imagined*, my editor said we needed a journal to go with it to really help people focus and keep track of their progress. So we created and published a companion journal.

Then the third book, *Single and Sixty,* was published. I am still working on getting *The Single Woman's Guide to Happiness* published.

I thought I had really expanded my comfort zone, but this was only the beginning!

Chapter Four

Traveling Through My Comfort Zone

By 2019, I had three published books under my belt, but I just didn't feel like I was making much of an impact.

Women over 50 were resonating with what I had to say, but I wanted to *do* more, *accomplish* more, and have a *bigger impact* on this segment of society because it seemed to me that other people of influence weren't putting much emphasis on them.

Traveling has always been one of my favorite adventures, and I had recently been on several trips with girlfriends and even traveled a bit in the United States by myself. This time, however, I wanted to do something bolder. I wanted to do something bigger. I wanted to really step out of my comfort zone.

I decided to attend a month-long conference in Croatia. It would be my first solo overseas trip.

Now comes the really interesting part: how I paid for the trip.

I didn't know exactly what it would cost and set my intentions on a certain amount. Since I didn't have the cash and I was continuing to simplify my life, I sold my tractor.

Attending the conference wasn't just a matter of coming up with the funds, there was also an application process.

How would little old me get accepted? Most attendees to previous conferences were decades younger. What would be so compelling about *me* that my acceptance would be assured? I knew I would have to do something outlandish to stand out. That's when I realized I would need to reveal more about my spiritual journey than I was comfortable sharing.

It was scary to claim I could connect to others telepathically, but I decided to go all out!

What the heck, my comfort zone was now a faint memory. I really wanted to go to the conference!

I sent in my application, not knowing if I would be accepted or even what the registration fee would be. People tried to talk me out of it by saying that I couldn't be away from home that long, it would cost too much, or I shouldn't travel alone. I kept a positive attitude and thought I would just figure things out.

I eagerly anticipated receiving official notification of acceptance. I really didn't have any doubts because I had done my very best.

When it came, I was so happy to be going!

Then I got the news informing me how much it would *really* cost! It was $1,500 more than I had planned.

I wasn't worried about the money, although I did not have it. Instead, I told myself, "I have been accepted, and I am already committed to going. I just need more money."

I put that request out to the Universe.

I had already figured out how I'd have someone manage my house, take care of my animals, get my bills paid, and take care of other work duties in my absence. I had actually been working toward this goal for a year, when the idea of living abroad for a month was first introduced to me.

At that point, the money was just a little bump in the road, not a big deal.

Guess what? A week later, I got a Costco rebate check for exactly that amount!

It was amazing. This confirmed my belief that the Universe sends us what we want when we need it. It all has to do with setting our intentions and being on the right vibration.

The Universe will bring us what we need.

It continued to deliver in Pula, Croatia, where I met other authors who were launching a compilation book while we were there. Most of them were first-time authors who had never published a book. They were so excited and invigorated, knowing they were now internationally published authors!

The thought of being part of an international book was exciting; however, they didn't have an upcoming topic that was a good fit for me. I did keep in contact with the publisher and a few authors through social media once I returned home.

Within a month, I received an email about an upcoming compilation book on travel. "Wow!" I thought, "Travel—that's my thing. I love traveling."

I quickly signed up and started the process of contributing to that book.

The theme of the book was how travel sparked our "ignite moment" and changed our life. Most of my trips were as a tourist, just seeing the sites, enjoying the food and experiencing the culture.

Wherever I went, I really learned to embrace all sorts of people and their way of living. In fact, I thought that was the greatest benefit of traveling.

Once again, I decided to expand far outside my comfort zone and reveal my most life-changing travel experience.

You see, for a time I'd been having conversations with people who were no longer in our earthly dimension, including departed loved ones and even people I had never met.

I thought I was truly connecting to these individuals, but it was difficult to get confirmation. I thought, well, maybe I can, or maybe I can't. Maybe this is just my imagination, or maybe I'm just freaking crazy!

Then ... I went to Egypt.

It was there that I decided to put this ability to the test. I was able to connect with departed souls that were well-known in Egyptian culture, such as Muhammad Ali. (No, not the American boxer.) This Muhammad Ali was revered as the founder of modern Egypt!

I also connected to slaves (which was a bit disconcerting), Ramesses the Great, and Nefertari (Ramesses's first royal wife).

These conversations solidified my own belief that I was genuinely able to make these connections.

Once I accepted my abilities, there was no going back. Mind you, I was quite terrified and thought, "Oh my gosh, if anybody knows what I'm really putting in here, the secret's going to be out; the cat's going to be out of the bag, and I'm going to be ostracized and disowned, and my family is going to have me committed!"

And then I thought, "Well, it's a good platform. It's not an entire book only about my story. The chances of anybody even reading my part are pretty slim. So, I'm just going to go for it."

What transpired totally amazed me.

First of all, the editors were quite in tune with these kinds of experiences. It wasn't a shock to them, and they were very encouraging. For that, I was very thankful.

When we launched the book, I met 30 other contributors. The publisher, JB Owen, made us stand up in front of everyone and share our story, which was a very frightening thing for me to do.

It's one thing to write a book that would be hidden away in somebody's library, never to be read. It's quite another to stand up in front of people and say, "Oh yeah … I talk to dead people."

I did it because I had to, and I was further pushed outside my comfort zone. I expected everyone to be surprised by my revelation, but they weren't! In fact, many of them told me they had similar experiences. It wasn't odd to them at all.

Oh my gosh, where were these people?

These were my peeps, as they say, certainly not the people I was hanging around with back home. That was helpful, and it gave me a little bit more confidence in accepting my abilities.

In my chapter of *Ignite Your Adventurous Spirit*, I came clean. I had to admit to myself that, yes, I can do this.

There was no more running from the truth. That was my "ignite" moment.

I also believed that others could do it, too, which was interesting because, in that book, there was a requirement to explain how others could do whatever we wrote about. Luckily, I didn't know of this requirement until late in the writing process, or I might not have signed up! My task was to put into words how other people might be able to connect with spiritual beings in a different dimension.

That book became an international bestseller in 12 countries, which was a super accomplishment and one for which I am eternally grateful because now I have bragging rights!

Little did I know this was merely a stepping stone to my final mission!

Chapter Five

Acknowledging My Final Mission

Where does that lead me today? Well, I *accepted* I could do this "connecting."

This was a key realization to me because I had actually already written another book—a very important book.

That book is called *The New I AM Document, Volume I*.

In 2019, during my meditation time, my spirit guides told me to be prepared with good pens and paper on hand because they were going to be giving me a book to write down.

This was a book I needed to get out to the world. In fact, they told me this book was my life's mission.

I jokingly said, "Well, I thought writing the women's books was my mission."

They responded, "No, that was just practice."

I must add that it was not meant in a negative way. It was meant as an explanation that we all have to start somewhere and then hone our skills.

My guides said my previous books were preparation for my next assignment, which would be given to me by ascended masters.

This new assignment would be to transcribe *The New I AM Document*, of which there would be three discourses. The ascended masters told me what to call the book, and soon enough, they started waking me up between two and three in the morning and asking me to get up to transcribe.

Initially, it was really hard because I kept falling asleep. I would try to write, but I couldn't get the messages quite right and would fall asleep while sitting in my chair.

They would even spell some words to me because I couldn't understand them. I got in the routine of going to bed, waking up, getting up and writing the lessons, and then I would go back to sleep.

Discerning the words for these lessons and writing them out by hand took all my energy. There was nothing left to evaluate their worthiness. Honestly, I barely remembered what I had written, so when I woke up the next morning, I'd go back and read it. I was astounded and thought, "Oh my gosh, this makes sense!"

When you read the book, you'll note that the names of the lessons seem rather strange at times. I remember thinking during the dictation or transcription, "How are you going to make a lesson or a story out of that?" but sure enough, they did.

I knew that I could not possibly be making this up because there were things in the book that I'd never heard of, never dreamt of, and were hard to even fathom.

For instance, in the very beginning of the book, it explains why we are here and that God created the world for us as a playground to learn and grow. Okay, that part sounds feasible, but the other information was more involved.

The book explains how we need to help each other learn these lessons so we can all ascend. And later, once everyone has learned the lessons and everyone has ascended, God will destroy the Earth. Furthermore, we will go to another place, like another planet, and repeat the process.

Now, that part blew my mind! Maybe others won't blink at that revelation, but I thought, "What the heck?"

Even though it was shocking to me, I just went with it. I reminded myself of the saying, "Don't shoot the messenger," and just wrote down the message.

I kept pressing on.

Eventually, I begged my guides, "Look, I'm happy to do this writing, but please I don't want to be woken up in the middle of the night for the rest of my life doing these three discourses. How am I ever going to get a boyfriend or a husband? Am I going to say, 'Oh yeah, well, excuse me. I just get up every night for two hours and write, and then I come back to bed. But other than that, I'm normal.'"

Yeah, right.

We worked out a deal where they would wake me up around five in the morning and I would write. By then, I was getting better at "connecting" to receive their messages.

This commitment led to the completion of the entire 100 lessons, followed by a question relating to the title, *The New I AM Document, Volume I.*

It was only later that I learned about *The I Am Discourses* by Guy W. Ballard in the 1930's. His books were downloaded from conversations with Saint Germain. I had never heard of these books, but it explains why I was told to include the word "new."

I wondered what my life would be like while I carried out my final mission.

Chapter Six

Connecting and Asking My Spirit Guides

Today, my life *is* quite different; it's a new way of living.

I can feel, sense, and understand how humans are connected to everything. Even though I am walking around and interacting with others and it appears I am the same as everyone else, I do not "feel" the same. I feel "connected."

I call it being connected to "All That Is." In such a scenario, one understands how everything we do has some effect on others and vice versa. I "feel" a sense of "connectedness" to everything.

This connectedness has led to great understanding.

I have asked so many questions over the last few years! I remember once asking my guides, "Why does it seem like sometimes it is one person (or being) that answers me and, other times, it seems like somebody else? They have a different tone, a different demeanor, and they use different words. It can't possibly be the same person (or being)."

My guides explained that it depends on the question asked and that the most appropriate person answers the question. This seemed incredible, so I said, "Oh, wow! It's like a giant Google."

They chuckled and said, "Yes, it is." I thought that was pretty cool. Just imagine being able to ask whatever pressing question you have!

What I've learned is that we *are* all connected in more ways than most of mankind can even fathom at this time in human development. And yes, we all have spirit guides. In fact, I've been told it's our job, even our duty, to ask our guides questions. They are not allowed to help us unless we *ask*.

That's why there are books such as *Ask and It is Given* by Esther Hicks, because truly we have to ask!

Thank goodness, I've always asked a lot of questions. It was a really good thing in my favor and helped with my spiritual growth. Of course, it is also helpful to get answers.

Many of us go through life asking questions, but not of the right people! We need to learn to go within and ask our spirit guides, although there are some helpers along the way.

Spirit guides are assigned to you for life. If you don't take advantage of this opportunity and ask your guides questions, your advancement will be much slower.

Additionally, if you won't ask for yourself, then ask for the benefit of your guides because they wait *our* entire lives to help us.

Can you imagine having a job and then never being called to do it? You might want to know it gives our guides immense joy to help all of us humans on our journey through this lifetime.

Being "connected" can bring us such understanding and growth! Can *you* imagine what you might learn from such connections?

Chapter Seven

Uncovering Past Lives Through Love

L ove is the most powerful force in the Universe.

We have all heard songs about how love can move mountains, and, in essence, it can. People will do anything for love, including completing tremendous feats or even dying for their loved ones. Elaborate monuments have been built in the memory of loved ones.

What one will do for love is literally limitless!

One important teaching about love is that it never dies. It is merely transformed.

Let me explain how this works. Let's say someone is married for a long time and they truly love their spouse with all their heart. Then things happen; their lives change, and they are no longer in love with that person. And maybe even for a while, their love turns to hate.

Maybe they're going through a bitter divorce, or there are child custody issues.

But later, that love will turn to something else, such as dismay or disappointment. Then eventually it'll change again to acceptance or mutual respect.

That's just an example. I'm sure we can all draw on our own lives to see how this has occurred.

But what I found most interesting was the concept that *love goes through timelines and dimensions*. I wrote a book that is yet to be published that goes into greater detail, but for now I would like to give you a glimpse.

There was a time when I was dating that I met someone, and we seemed to have so much in common. It was a bit eerie, but I didn't even wonder why because I was so caught up in the moment.

I was just over the moon and finally realized that I was crazy in love with this man. (Much more so than either of my former husbands!)

He would share very private thoughts, which surprised me. These weren't things you would normally say out loud. When it first happened, I just thought, well, he's being pretty honest. It wasn't until later that I realized I didn't actually see his lips move.

It had to be his inner thoughts! I could *hear* his thoughts! I could hear his whispers.

It took months to realize that I was picking up on his subconscious or inner thoughts.

Then the dream started again.

Twenty years ago, I had a recurring dream. After meeting this man, the dream returned. Each time I dreamed, it would continue a little further, much like a movie. I would wake up before I saw the end.

I could tell I was married, but I didn't actually see my spouse. At night before bed and during my morning meditation time, I kept asking, "Who is the man in the dream?"

Eventually, I saw his face, and it *was* the man I had dated.

Through additional visions and dreams, I realized we had an entire lifetime together.

I found out many facts, such as where we lived at the time, my name, his name, the names of our 11 children, what religion we were, why we moved from one place to another, and even how we died.

It was fascinating! I have had additional visions and saw myself giving birth to our fourth child. Now, that is pretty amazing! (Good thing the vision didn't hurt.)

I couldn't figure out why I felt such a strong bond to this man, even after we were no longer seeing each other. I had been married before, but never had an attachment linger like this.

What I've found out is that not only does love never die, but it also goes through time and dimensions. My guides told me this repeatedly, and I have *felt* it.

I have since found out this man and I had several lifetimes together in different time periods and in different locations. With one of the lifetimes, I even thought, "Oh no, this can't be; my spirit guides are just playing tricks on me."

But eventually I saw numerous visions, and I researched the information I did obtain. This helped me to understand more fully.

The visions are like watching a bit of a movie. The movie starts, and you just see one scene. Then after a while you put the pieces together.

When I'm having these visions, I ask so many questions that I have to remind myself to quit asking questions and pay attention to the dream or the vision and just enjoy it!

These experiences have totally solidified my belief in past lives and the fact that we do, indeed, recognize people from previous lifetimes.

When my journey began, just the idea of reincarnation was new to me! But now I truly believe it because I have seen so many of my lives. Doubtful at first, I researched things I learned during my visions, and they fit the time and historical facts. (See how having an inquisitive mind is helpful?)

I often asked how one or both of us died or about our children. I was very curious. But it wasn't just entertainment. My past lives held so much information that has been helpful in *this* lifetime.

There were unpleasant things in my past lives, such as being hungry, homeless, freezing cold, losing a child, my husband dying, and other unfortunate occurrences. Why would I want to relive all this suffering? The reason lies in the lessons learned.

My greatest lesson was how a loving marriage should be. I am most grateful for this understanding. These were the types of marriages that I imagined for this lifetime but did not occur. I just never could understand why.

My past lives helped me understand, and it has left me with such peace I cannot even explain.

After my experiences, I do believe that we have these connections with other people. Once I was approached by a girlfriend who said she "felt a bond with me." So I asked my guides, and it was true. In fact, she helped me give birth to several children in one of my lifetimes!

Furthermore, I've done a little research on past lives and begun to listen to others more carefully. There are many people who *do* believe in past lives, even people you may already know!

Some believe we incarnate in "soul groups" or our own little tribe, and we change roles. At times, we might be the parent and they might be the child, or we might be brothers and sisters, but we are all there to help each other learn these lessons.

This is why when we meet some people, we think we recognize them or feel comfortable with them right off the bat. These are often people from our soul group.

For me, it was like that with this man. I just didn't know what it was. Why did I feel like I could tell him anything, and why did it feel like I'd known him my whole life?

I certainly didn't feel that way with my two former husbands. With them, I was not free to say what I felt, and I was not valued. I knew I couldn't be myself. But with him, I could truly be myself without any repercussions.

Knowing that someone else accepted me just as I am seemed to be a pivotal point in my spiritual journey. It was that *knowing* that helped me have faith in myself, put doubt aside, and accept that our life here on Earth is, indeed, limitless!

Chapter Eight

Exploring The New I AM Document, Volume I

Is The New I AM Document giving you all the answers to life in one easy-to-understand book?

It is, and it isn't. Volume I is merely the first layer in this journey. (Remember, there will be three volumes.)

The depth of the lessons became clear to me once the downloads started. Some of the topics are revisited even within this book so that one can gain a better understanding. I believe that is how our "education" will unfold.

Think of it this way: simple lessons, expounded upon, with additional lessons leading to a fuller understanding of the meaning and purpose of life.

This book is a discourse from ascended masters, which gives an explanation of what our journey on Earth is all about. There are a hundred lessons that we are here to learn.

Keep in mind, this is only the first discourse.

Volume I can be described as part of a larger body of knowledge, similar to one of the books in the Bible. The New I AM Document is not geared only to Christians or those who follow the Bible. It can be, but it applies to any religion because they all lead to the same place. They just have a different way of teaching because different cultures accept religion in their own ways.

For instance, Native Americans learned religion through stories passed down from generation to generation. They were taught a lot about the environment and cohabitating with nature. Actually, that is what is taught in The New I AM Document—about how we're all connected and we're all One.

Other people have their own religion, specific to their culture, such as Islam. Contrary to the belief that some people in the U.S. spread about Muslims, they are not evil and hateful! They are quite loving people.

They have sayings such as, "Allah will provide," which is almost verbatim to the Bible.

I remember the first time I heard someone say that.

When we lived in Izmir, Turkey, our kapıçi (building manager of our apartment building) invited us to his home. He, his wife, and newborn baby had a tiny one-room apartment at the top of a neighboring building. I thought, "How can he be so happy and so sure Allah would provide?"

Living in such meager surroundings, it didn't make sense to me.

Now, I understand it is a matter of realizing there is a greater power and letting go of our own ego and learning to embrace the higher power.

It's a matter of turning over our worries and fears to someone (or something else) and trusting life will unfold to our best interest. It is literally freeing to let go!

When you read The New I AM Document, wherever it says the word "God," you can substitute your own higher power (Allah, Buddha, or Jesus).

Feel free to use the words "Source" or "The Universe" if you don't associate with any specific religious group.

This book can serve as a supplement to one's own religious books, giving easy-to-understand explanations for how we are to live as a human species. It also speaks to those who don't feel comfortable with any specific or standard religion.

There is no intent to steal people away from other religions by saying, "This is the *only* way!"

You see, there is no one way.

There are as many different ways to God-consciousness as there are religions because everybody has their own version. Even two Catholics have different interpretations and follow the rules differently.

The main concept of the book is that we are all *connected* and, therefore, WE ARE ALL ONE, part of the same consciousness.

This book helps people learn the lessons necessary to live such a life.

The lessons are presented in such a simple manner that when you hear them, you might think, "Oh yeah, I know that."

But the question really is, "Are you *living* it?"

Perhaps we all need some reinforcement, because truly everyone in the world is *not* doing everything in this book.

If we were all acting in accordance with these lessons, we would all be ascended beings. We would also be in the next level of consciousness that I write about in this book, where we have all elevated and are ready for the next iteration in a new location.

It will take some time for complete understanding. The lessons we need to understand are that things happen for a reason and we don't always get what we want from God.

We should know that God always hears our request … and sometimes it's granted, and sometimes it's not. Other times, it just hasn't been granted *yet*.

There's a story I just love that exemplifies this lesson! There was a young woman who thought she had met the love of her life. She implored God to let her be with this man. God kept saying, "No, he's not ready."

In other words, the man needed to do some growing first. The man wasn't worthy to be with her at the time, as he still had lessons to learn.

But the woman kept begging and begging. So finally, God (tired of her whining and wanting to teach *her* a lesson) let her be with this man.

What she learned was that God wasn't kidding when He said he wasn't ready—and her life was miserable. Only then did she realize God was right, and she should have listened.

If you are like this person and you don't get who you want, you might want to realize they are not ready. Perhaps they need to grow, and maybe *you* need to grow, too.

When the time is right, when both parties are ready, maybe you will meet again and have a relationship.

It's important for us as humans to understand that all will be done in God's perfect timing, not ours. This is so very difficult for humans because we want it, and we want it *now!* And that's all there is to this story, but it's not the *end* of the story.

This story has multiple layers. The obvious one is listening to God, but we also need to trust God and wait for *His* timing. It's a great lesson in patience, too. So, you see, there are lots of stories exemplifying the lessons we need to learn.

Not only will you learn how to be a better person, but you can use it as a way to *reinforce* your religion, *evolve* in your religion, or even *create* your own religion. Religion is merely one pathway to give us guidance for adopting our own inner belief system.

This inner belief or guidance system gets us one step closer to ascension, the final goal of mankind.

Chapter Nine

Unlocking the Key to Ascension

The importance of *feelings* cannot be underestimated.

What I've come to learn is that we all have an inner guidance system. Esther Hicks is known for this concept.

Some people call it intuition. Some people call it higher self, and you may have another name. It's that "gut feeling" we have about something.

This is the key to unlocking our best life, and it leads us on the path to ascension (higher consciousness).

Have you ever had an instance when somebody asked you to do something and you had a gut feeling it was wrong, but you did it anyway? Then later you think, "Man, I wish I wouldn't have done that!"

We need to learn to trust our gut feelings, our intuition, our instincts, or our guidance system. If you learn to get in touch with your feelings (your *inner* feelings) and then act in accordance with them, your life will change dramatically for the better.

You see, inside all of us is love for everyone and everything, and even *more* love, kindness, and joy. We need to be conscious and mindful of it, so that when we are deciding about how to behave in our lives, we act in congruence with how we *feel* inside.

In other words, internally, we feel a love and kindness toward others. But if we are upset about what someone does, our first impulse might be to yell at them and say, "You stupid idiot!"

When we do that, we usually feel bad afterwards. That's because our actions don't match our inner guidance system.

We all need to learn how to act in congruence.

The first way to do this is to *recognize* that we are not behaving properly. Then we need to recognize when we *feel* bad about our actions. If we lash out at someone, we need to see what we have done, understand that we lashed out and that doing so is unnecessary.

At first, you are *aware* of your poor actions, but you act out of habit and do it anyway. Later, you get better at realizing what you are about to do, and you tell yourself, "I'm going to stop myself this time. I'm not going to lash out and say something inappropriate."

The next time you recognize it, and you don't lash out. Instead of saying nothing, you say something kind and encouraging.

Through practice, you will get to the point that when these trying times come up, you will not lash out in anger or frustration, but only respond with loving kindness.

Eventually, it will become a normal way of being.

Once you start living the lessons that are in this book, you will become a better human and, someday, an ascended being.

Don't worry! You do not have to die to be ascended.

You will be on Earth, walking around, interacting with other people, but it's as if your soul is in a different dimension, which gives you a better understanding of everything. You are still physical, but you're also operating in that other realm simultaneously.

It can be a hard concept to understand, but if you go within for answers, you can attain comprehension!

By paying attention to your feelings, you will learn how to act in congruence.

Mastering oneself and learning the lessons and operating from a place of love and peace will bring so much joy and happiness to your life. It's a totally different way to operate. It's like getting a 10X upgrade to your operating system, making you more aware and alert.

You *will* be a loving person.

You *will* be ascended.

You *will* literally be a light for others.

People *will* come up to you and say, "How did you do that? You seem so happy, and you're so different." Accepting those sorts of comments will become second nature.

It *will* become your normal state of existence.

This is what I wish for you and everyone else.

This is why I want people to read this book, learn from it, and grow from it.

Together, we can all help humanity rise to the level of consciousness our Creator has envisioned.

Bonus Excerpt from The New I AM Document – Volume I

Available on Amazon

www.TheNewIAMMovement.com/volume1

BONUS: BOOK EXCERPT

Greetings, fellow mankind. My name is Janie J and I am a "medium" or "channeler."

For those of you unfamiliar with what that means (like I used to be), it means I am able to connect between the spirit realm, which we can sense but not see, and our physical world here on Earth.

I learned how to do this a few years ago when I kept asking and trying to connect to a very special person in my life. I had no idea that such a deep desire would have this outcome!

I have used this gift to connect to many souls—living and deceased—in order to gain understanding and to help them and their families. This ability can be "turned on" quite easily by simply asking them.

Other times it can be a bit intrusive and I can hear or sense these souls speaking to me without provocation on my part.

I believe they can tell I'm an open channel and able to sense their feelings. Again, it is quite informative. I have learned many important lessons this way.

[Editor's Note: You can learn this method by down-loading the author's Connect to Transform Process™ PDF for free at www.TheNewIAMMovement.com/transform] At the end of 2016, I was told to write three books, which I did along with strict deadlines. However, the publishing of those books was a bit slow on the execution. The purpose of these books is to encourage women to live their best lives.

Another book is also in the making, designed to open up women to the possibility of a spiritual life – for living one's best life does indeed include spirituality, which is nothing more than the understanding that there is more to life than what we experience in the physical world here on Earth.

In early 2019, I was given my final life's mission. (Yes, we *really* do have one!) That mission is to transcribe a document that is known as, "The New I AM Document."

By transcription, I mean, I sit quietly and these words, these teachings, come to me from above…from Ascended Masters (or Archangels) assisting God. This book is the first of three discourses.

This mission will carry me through until the end of my earthly life—into my late 90's.

It's important to know that as a child I received very little religious training. Often, I would sense "right or wrong," yet it would be nothing specifically learned from my parents.

An example I remember vividly is being in middle school where social cliques were prevalent. To talk to an outsider was reason for you to be excluded, which I quickly discovered.

This never seemed "right" to me. I know now that this lesson was embedded inside me when I began life on Earth.

Another long-held belief of mine has been that it doesn't matter if you succeed on a specific task. It matters most that you try your best. This belief was not instilled in me by my parents or teachers. Now I know this belief also came with me, as you will learn the same lesson in this book many times.

I ask that you listen carefully with an open mind and an open heart, to my transcriptions.

Absorb them into your being and strive to teach others through your actions and words, so that someday all mankind will be lifted up to a new way of life, a new reality where we are all truly and deeply connected *and* aware of such connectedness.

Be well. Be love. Be the light.

Janie J

Lesson 1 - **The Purpose**

In the beginning, God created the Heavens and Earth as a playground, much like a classroom for mankind to learn and grow, to become all he/she can be.

The purpose was the growth or Ascension of mankind to the next level of evolution where all men/women are all-knowing and very much aware of their connectedness to each other and to the Earth—to include the environment and all the animals. We *are* all truly connected as One; much, much more than the individual man knows at this moment.

All mankind has different issues to handle or solve. We must work together to consciously and subconsciously solve these issues. Part of what we need to learn is how to work together—as One. The point of this entire exercise is that we *are* One, so we must learn to act as one cohesive unit. All mankind is One. One with each other and One with God.

It's the most important lesson we are here to learn.

With the help of you and many others, God's plan is to raise the planet's shared consciousness to a new level, never known before. A level where we all can experience the glory of an earthly life well before we ascend to the Heavens and someday to another solar system (an alternate Universe).

It will be much the same as this one—a playground for our enjoyment and eventual growth. This is a repeating pattern in the Universe. One that mankind is not yet aware of. With your help and that of our other Ascended Masters though, someday all mankind will know and experience this type of monumental growth.

Join The New I AM Movement

Are you ready to change your life for the better?

Are you ready to upgrade your existence?

Are you ready to help move mankind to a higher level of consciousness that is in line with what our Creator envisioned?

It all starts with YOU!

If you are ready to take the first step on this spiritual journey, find out how to get these lessons so you can grow into a *better person,* connect to the source and become a *more evolved spiritual being.*

Start your journey by going to:
www.TheNewIAmMovement.com/transform

Just imagine being a part of this extraordinary movement — a movement to move mankind ahead to new, higher levels of understanding and consciousness. Such a noble feat is quite possible if we work *together* to make this happen!

Join The New I AM Movement as you work on your own spiritual development.

Connect to me, to others, your higher self, and with your spirit guides, ascended masters, and universal intelligence.

We are all available to help you on your spiritual journey.

About Janie Jurkovich

Photo by Signature Creations Photography

Janie Jurkovich (known as Janie J) is an author, nationally-ranked athlete, world traveler, and a spirit medium.

Her first book, *Live The Life You Have Imagined*, outlines the steps necessary to live your best life.

Her second publication was a companion journal.

Her third book, *Single and Sixty*, which reached Amazon Bestseller status when released, is an inspirational and humorous account of her life after she became suddenly divorced after a long marriage.

Her fourth literary publication was as a contributor to a compilation book, *Ignite Your Adventurous Spirit,* which reached International Bestseller status on Amazon in 12 countries. Her chapter tells of a trip to Egypt where her spiritual gifts and connecting abilities could no longer be denied.

Her next book, *The New I AM Document, Volume I*, will be released in 2021. She downloaded this life-changing discourse from ascended masters in 2019.

The book answers the big questions in life: why we are here on Earth and what we are to learn.

Find out more at www.TheNewIAmMovement.com.

After embracing her "gift" of connecting to souls in other realms, she has committed her life to helping others by sharing what she has learned.

Her life goal is to help lift the consciousness of all mankind.

Ms. Jurkovich lives in the country near Clovis, California with her dog, Pepper, a brood of hens, and a flock of sheep. It's a tranquil setting which allows her to connect to the spirit world so she can live her life's purpose.

Contact:

www.TheNewIAmMovement.com

www.JanieJ.net

Phone: 559-295-2500

Notes

Notes

www.ingramcontent.com/pod-product-compliance
Lightning Source LLC
Chambersburg PA
CBHW062150100526
44589CB00014B/1769